THEMATIC UNIT
ANCIENT GREECE

Written by David Jefferies

Illustrated by Cheryl Buhler

Teacher Created Materials, Inc.
6421 Industry Way
Westminster, CA 92683
www.teachercreated.com
©1993 Teacher Created Materials, Inc.
Reprinted, 2003
Made in U.S.A.
ISBN 1-55734-297-0

D0018443

Table of Contents

Introduction

Greek civilization has made important and lasting contributions to the culture of our country and the entire world. Situated as it is in the Mediterranean, it absorbed the influences of Asia, Africa and Europe and produced a culture that made important contributions to art, literature, science, philosophy, politics—to every aspect of human life. This unit attempts to avoid reducing this culture to a litany of dates and lives of famous men. In the spirit of a whole language philosophy, the unit gives the students a chance to actively experience some aspects of the culture they are studying. A basic historical framework is given through a time line and study of city states. The mythology is studied at some depth, but the study of every cluster of myths is carried through to a study of Greek history, geography and thought. The second half of the unit studies aspects of Greek history and gives students an idea of how people actually lived in the ancient Greek culture.

This thematic unit includes:

❏ **literature selections**—summaries of two children's books with related lessons (complete with reproducible pages) that cross the curriculum

❏ **language experience and writing ideas**—suggestions as well as activities across the curriculum, including Big Books

❏ **bulletin board ideas**—suggestions and plans for student-created and/or interactive bulletin boards

❏ **homework suggestions**—extending the unit to the child's home

❏ **curriculum connections**—in language arts, math, science, art, history, and life skills such as cooking and physical education

❏ **group projects**—to foster cooperative learning

❏ **culminating activities**—which require students to synthesize their learning to produce a product or engage in an activity that can be shared with others

❏ **a bibliography**—suggesting additional literature and nonfiction books on the theme

---

To keep this valuable resource intact so that it can be used year after year, you may wish to punch holes in the pages and store them in a three-ring binder.

Introduction *(cont.)*

Why Whole Language?

A whole language approach involves children in using all modes of communication: reading, writing, listening, observing, illustrating, experiencing, and doing. Communication skills are interconnected and integrated into lessons that emphasize the whole of language rather than isolating its parts. The lessons revolve around selected literature. Reading is not taught as a separate subject from writing and spelling, for example. A child reads, writes (spelling appropriately for his/her level), speaks, listens, etc., in response to a literature experience introduced by the teacher. In this way, language skills grow naturally, stimulated by involvement and interest in the topic at hand.

Why Thematic Planning?

One very useful tool for implementing an integrated whole language program is thematic planning. By choosing a theme with correlating literature selections for a unit of study, a teacher can plan activities throughout the day that lead to a cohesive, in-depth study of the topic. Students will be practicing and applying their skills in meaningful contexts. Consequently, they will tend to learn and retain more. Both teachers and students will be freed from a day that is broken into unrelated segments of isolated drill and practice.

Why Cooperative Learning?

Besides academic skills and content, students need to learn social skills. No longer can this area of development be taken for granted. Students must learn to work cooperatively in groups in order to function well in modern society. Group activities should be a regular part of school life, and teachers should consciously include social objectives as well as academic objectives in their planning. For example, a group working together to solve a problem may need to select a leader. The teacher should make clear to the students and monitor the qualities of good leader-follower group interaction just as he/she would state and monitor the academic goals of the project.

Why Big Books?

An excellent cooperative, whole language activity is the production of Big Books. Groups of students, or the whole class, can apply their language skills, content knowledge, and creativity to produce a Big Book that can become a part of the classroom library to be read and reread. These books make excellent culminating projects for sharing beyond the classroom with parents, librarians, other classes, etc. Big Books can be produced in many ways, and this thematic unit book includes directions for at least one method you may choose.

Greek Mythology

Summary

The myths in this thematic unit are sequenced in a rough chronological order. The first day is about creation and societies' beginnings. The next day deals with the earliest historical period, the Minoan. Hercules and Jason are of the generation before the Homeric period (in fact, it is said that Achilles was a boy when Hercules sailed with Jason and the Argonauts). The Iliad and The Odyssey create a bridge between the mythical/heroic age of Grecian thought and the historical, which the second half of the unit will deal with in more detail.

The following is a suggested plan for the myth section of the unit.

Sample Plan

Day 1
- Stories of Creation and the Myth of Prometheus
- Daily Writing Activities (page 41)
- Read Creation and Prometheus stories
- Prometheus: Creator of the Human Race (page 9)
- Introducing the Olympian Gods (page 10)
- Cinquain for the Gods (page 42)

Day 2
- Myths of the Labyrinth and Theseus
- Daily writing activities
- Read myths of Daedalus and Theseus
- The Ancient Land of Crete (page 13)
- Building a Labyrinth (page 14)
- A Collection of Monsters (page 15)

Day 3
- Myth of Demeter and Persephone
- Daily writing activities
- Read myths of Demeter and Persephone
- Myth and Emotions (page 17)
- The Climate of Greece and the Aegean Islands (page 16)
- Seeds of Persephone (page 47)
- Investigating Three Grains (page 60)
- Continue games with Olympian Gods (page 10)
- Grain Art (page 65)

Day 4
- The Search for the Golden Fleece
- Continue daily writing activities
- Read myths of Hercules and/or Jason
- Looking for the Hero (page 18)
- Heracles and the Hydra (page 48)
- Eyes of the Monster (page 49)

- Continue games with Olympian Gods (page 10)
- Eyes and Greek Art (page 65)

Day 5
- *The Iliad*
- Continue daily writing activities
- Read the first half of *The Iliad*
- A Series of Duels (page 20)
- Greek Writing (page 19)
- Begin Big Book of the Gods (page 26)

Day 6
- *The Iliad*
- Continue daily writing activities
- Read the second half of *The Iliad*
- Fact and Fiction in *The Iliad* (page 21)
- Illustrating a Passage (page 22)
- The Shield of Agamemnon (page 65)
- Continue Big Book of the Gods

Day 7
- *The Odyssey*
- Continue daily writing activities
- Read the first half of *The Odyssey*
- The Wily Odysseus (page 23)
- A Comb for the Cyclops (page 50)
- Begin Making a Greek Town (page 77)

Day 8
- *The Odyssey*
- Continue daily writing activities
- Read second half of *The Odyssey*
- Using Tableaux to Explore Meaning (page 24)
- Continue Making a Greek Town
- Finish Big Book of the Gods

Overview of Activities

Source Books for Mythology and Legends

The stories of Greek mythology are available in many versions and editions, no one unit is specified. Instead, it focuses on one myth or legend for each day (except for allowing two days each for *The Iliad* and *The Odyssey*). The list below supplies you with a number of sources for each myth, but the list is not meant to be exhaustive. Whatever version of the story you find will most likely contain the same basic incidents. If you find multiple versions that differ, so much the better. The mythology of the Greeks varied in time and across space, because the Greeks themselves did not all tell the exact same version of the myth.

Guidelines for Teaching the Myths

A set up for preparing, enjoying, and extending each myth is included in this overview. Following these steps when teaching each myth will allow for a comprehensive learning experience for students.

The bibliographic entries below are followed by an annotation that will tell which myths the books contain.

Connolly, Peter. *The Legend of Odysseus.* (Oxford University Press, 1986)
    A complete treatment of both *The Iliad* and *The Odyssey*, with numerous historical and cultural connections to the stories.

D'Aulaire, Ingri and Edgar. *D'Aulaires' Book of Greek Myths.* (Doubleday, 1962)
    Creation story and Prometheus, Demeter, Theseus, Heracles, and an abbreviated version of *The Iliad.*

Evslin, Bernard. *The Greek Gods.* (Scholastic, 1966). Creation and Prometheus, Demeter.

Evslin, Bernard, et. al. *Heroes and Monsters of Greek Myth.* (Scholastic, 1967). A full treatment of both Daedalus and Theseus.

Hutton, Warwick. *Theseus and the Minotaur.* (Margaret McElderry Books, 1989). Contains only the Theseus part of the story.

Alexander, Beatrice. *Famous Myths of the Golden Age.* (Random House, 1947). Prometheus (not the creations section), Demeter, Persephone and an abbreviated version of *The Odyssey.*

Guidelines for Teaching *The Iliad* and *The Odyssey*

This unit has been written with the idea of using the Peter Connolly version of the epics, which combines reading selections of a manageable length and pages devoted to historical and cultural aspects of the Greek heroic age.

However, using that book is not a requirement. If it is not available, you might also use a number of shorter versions to provide students with a sense of the richness of the stories. Material from encyclopedias and other non-fiction materials about the art, dress and culture of the Heroic Age will help supply students with a historical context.

If you use Connolly's book, sequence the reading as follows:

Day 5:   Chapters 1 and 2, "All Because of a Girl" and "Days of Death"

Day 6:   Chapter 3, "Days of Sorrow"

Day 7:   Chapter 4, "The Great Adventure"

Day 8:   Chapter 5, "The Homecoming"

Overview of Activities *(cont.)*

PROMETHEUS

Preparing: If you can find other creation myths from other cultures, read them to the class before you read the Greek version. Discuss how humankind is created in each.

Enjoying: Read the myth of Prometheus. Distribute "Prometheus: Creator of the Human Race" (page 9). Make clay, paper, craft sticks, wire and other items available for creating human shapes.

Extending: Explain that the Greeks prayed to many different gods and goddesses. Their deities had different characteristics and various powers. Many of them were members of the same family. They were called the Olympians. Distribute the materials for "Introducing the Olympian Gods" and play one of the games on page 10.

THESEUS, THE MINOTAUR AND THE LABYRINTH

Preparing: Explain that the Minoan culture was even earlier than the Greek culture. The Minoans influenced many things in the Greek culture. Ask what a labyrinth (or maze) is and discuss the students' ideas. Explain that this story has a famous labyrinth in it. Distribute "Building a Labyrinth" (page 14) and give students time to make their own. Ask a few students to present theirs to the class.

Enjoying: After reading the story, distribute "The Ancient Land of Crete" (page 13). Read the information. Ask the students to form groups to answer the question at the bottom of the page. Give groups time to compare their answers.

Extending: Discuss the idea of the Minotaur. Why is he a monster? Do they know any other stories in which different animals are combined to form an imaginary one. Then distribute "A Collection of Monsters" (page 15) and ask the students to match the verse with the picture. If time permits, allow students to draw their own combination monster. Ask them to write a verse to describe it.

DEMETER AND PERSEPHONE

Preparing: Explain that some myths helped to describe the world to the people who told them. Demeter was the goddess of grain. This story will tell something very important about how farmers grew crops. Greece has a climate that is called "Mediterranean." Distribute "The Climate of Greece and the Aegean Islands" (page 16) and complete the questions.

Enjoying: Read the myth and discuss its meaning. Distribute "Myth and the Emotions" (page 17). Give the students time to respond and compare their responses. Emphasize how impulsive the Greek deities seem to be.

Extending: Distribute "Persephone's Six Seeds" (page 47). Have beans or other manipulatives available. Continue your day with grains by using "Investigating Three Grains" (page 60). (Bird seed mixes often contain many types of grains.)

Overview of Activities *(cont.)*

MYTHS OF JASON AND THE ARGONAUTS

Introducing: Briefly discuss the idea of the hero and what it means to the students. Explain that many myths describe heroic acts that people performed, but that what people think of as heroic may change with time. Read the stories of Jason and/or Hercules.

Enjoying: Looking for the hero will help the students to answer the questions that you raised before you read the text.

Extending: Two math activities "Eyes of the Monster" (page 49) and "The Hydra" (page 48) will take incidents in the stories and explore their mathematical implications. The fact that many Greek ships had eyes painted on them (including the *Argo*) will help you set up "Eyes Everywhere" (page 65).

The Iliad

Introducing: Introduce the Homeric epics as one of the earliest examples of written storytelling. Explain that Homer might or might not refer to a real person. The epics might have been created by numerous singers over many centuries. Explain that many singers/poets would entertain people in villages and towns and that the story of Troy and how it was destroyed was the most popular story to them. Guide the students through "Greek Writing" (page 19) as a way of continuing this introduction.

Enjoying: After you have read half of the story, discuss what is happening Do the students see that pattern of battle like a series of single combats? Use "A Series of Duels" (page 20) as a way to widen this discussion. Guide the students to see that the logic of the story dictates that the climax of the story will be the two champions, Achilles and Hector, doing battle with each other. "Illustrating a Passage" (page 22) will help students understand the meanings of the second half of the epic.

Extending: Briefly discuss how important the gods are to the action of the story. Use "Big Book of the Gods" (page 26) as a way to extend not only *The Iliad*, but the whole section on mythology. "Fact and Fiction" in *The Iliad* (page 21) will continue the bridge between the mythology and history sections of the thematic unit.

The Odyssey

Introducing: Briefly discuss Odysseus' place in *The Iliad*. Explain that after *The Iliad* had been written, a second epic appeared, which was an adventure story about how Odysseus got home after wandering for ten years. The exercise "Making a Greek Town" (page 77) has applications beyond merely introducing *The Odyssey*, but you can use it to help the students change their focus from the mythology/history mixture of the Heroic Age to the thoroughly recorded history that makes up the second half of the unit.

Enjoying: Have students respond to "The Wily Odysseus" (page 23) to help them focus on the main character of the later epic. "Using Tabelaux to Explore Meaning" (pages 24 and 25) will help them understand the feelings and motivations of the characters.

Extending: "A Comb for the Cyclops" (page 50) will give students a chance to exercise their senses of proportion and scale.

Prometheus: Creator of the Human Race

In Greek mythology, it was Prometheus who at the command of Zeus created the human race. With the materials that your teacher gives you, pretend you are Prometheus. Create a human being from those materials.

Imagine that your human does not know how to use fire. What would his/her life be like without fire?

_____

_____

_____

_____

Write about how his/her life would change if he/she could use fire.

_____

_____

_____

_____

_____

The myth of Prometheus seems to be saying that it is the use of fire that allowed humans to lead lives vastly different from the ones that animals live. Do you agree or disagree? Explain your answer.

_____

_____

_____

_____

_____

_____

Introducing the Olympian Gods

The Olympians, the major Greek gods and goddesses, normally number twelve. If your students have read an account of the Greek creation myth, then they have read about the earlier generations of deities, about Uranus and Cronus and Rhea. If not, briefly explain that Zeus, although the most powerful of the Greeks gods, was not thought to be the creator of the world. Rather, the Greeks thought there had been several generations of gods, that Zeus himself had a mother, father, and also had a multitude of sons and daughters, some of them mortal, some immortal. Below are three games that will help establish some basic knowledge of the Greek pantheon.

Materials: copies of pages 11-12, cut out, backed with construction paper and laminated if possible.

Game 1: Olympian Concentration

Materials: one set of cards

Directions: Players lay out the cards in a six-by-four arrangement. Players try to turn over matching pairs (one information and one picture card), turning them back over when unsuccessful.

Game 2: Four Questions

Materials: one set of cards

Directions: Place cards face up in a row, information cards on top of picture cards. One player thinks of a card. The other may ask four yes-no questions about the information on the cards to try to find the identity of the deity chosen by the first player. The player who is asking the questions may sort the cards as he/she asks questions.

> **Name of God:** Zeus
> **Title:** King of the Gods, God of the Heavens
> **Parents:** Cronus and Rhea
> **Roman Name:** Jupiter
> **Animals/things sacred to him:** eagle, thunderbolt, shield, oak tree

Game 3: Attribute Game

Materials: one set of cards

Directions: One player gives directions for which cards to choose, making them as complicated as he/she wishes. (e.g., "Pick all female deities who have an emblem that is a bird but who is not a daughter of Zeus." [answer: Hera]). For added level of difficulty, play the game so that the person following the directions only sees the picture cards.

Information Game Cards

Name of God: Zeus
Title: King of the Gods, God of the Heavens
Parents: Cronus and Rhea
Roman Name: Jupiter
Animals/things sacred to him: eagle, thunderbolt, shield, oak tree

Name of Goddess: Aphrodite
Title: Goddess of Love and Beauty
Parents: Zeus and Dione
Roman Name: Venus
Animals/things sacred to her: dove, goose, sparrow, myrtle

Name of God: Poseidon
Title: God of the Sea
Parents: Cronus and Rhea
Roman Name: Neptune
Animals/things sacred to him: trident, horse, bull

Name of God: Ares
Title: God of War
Parents: Zeus and Hera
Roman Name: Mars
Animals/things sacred to him: vulture, dog

Name of God: Hades
Title: God of the Underworld
Parents: Cronus and Rhea
Roman Name: Pluto
Animals/things sacred to him: helmet, metal jewels

Name of God: Hephaestus
Title: God of the Forge
Parents: Zeus and Hera
Roman Name: Vulcan
Animals/things sacred to him: fire, blacksmith's hammer

Name of Goddess: Athena
Title: Goddess of Wisdom, of the City, of War, of Arts and Crafts
Parents: Zeus and Metis
Roman Name: Minerva
Animals/things sacred to her: owl, shield, olive tree

Name of God: Artemis
Title: Goddess of the Moon, the Hunt, of Children
Parents: Zeus and Leto
Roman Name: Diana
Animals/things sacred to her: stag, crescent moon, cypress

Name of God: Apollo
Title: God of Light and Truth, Healing, Archery, Music
Parents: Zeus and Leto
Roman Name: Apollo
Animals/things sacred to him: crow, dolphin, laurel, lyre

Name of Goddess: Demeter
Title: Goddess of the Harvest, of Agriculture
Parents: Cronus and Rhea
Roman Name: Ceres
Animals/things sacred to her: wheat

Name of Goddess: Hera
Title: Queen of the Gods
Parents: Cronus and Rhea
Roman Name: Juno
Animals/things sacred to her: peacock, cow

Name of God: Hermes
Title: God of Motion, Sleep and Dreams, Travellers, Thieves
Parents: Zeus and Maia
Roman Name: Mercury
Animals/things sacred to him: wand, winged sandals, winged helmet

Picture Game Cards

The Ancient Land of Crete

The first major seafaring civilization in the Mediterranean region was the Minoan Civilization (named after King Minos of the Theseus story). They began to sail across the eastern Mediterranean as early as 2500 B.C.)

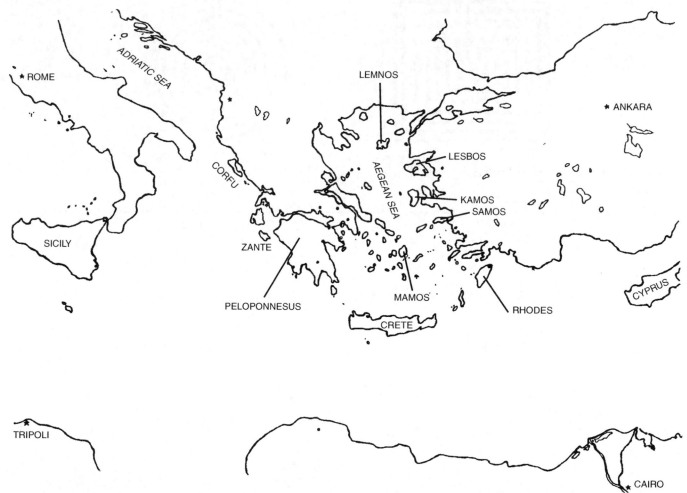

They were skilled architects, building large and complicated palaces and cities. One palace in particular was full of twisting and winding passages. They filled their palaces with beautiful pictures that today show us much about the way the people lived or thought. Some pictures show an arena where young men risked death by leaping over charging bulls. They were masters at making jewelry and pottery, and they developed a system of writing. Their most important city was called Knossus.

During this time, the Greeks had a very simple technology. It is believed that Minoans landed in Greece and colonized some parts of it. The Greeks who lived there imitated the Minoan style of architecture and pottery. Slowly the Minoan society became weaker and the Greeks (then called Mycenaeans) became stronger. Eventually the Mycenaeans landed in Crete and destroyed Knossus. The Mycenaeans took control of the eastern part of the Mediterranean.

After you have finished reading the Theseus myth and the information, answer the following. One explanation of the Theseus myth is that it is a kind of history, a story about how the Greeks were first under the control of the Minoans, and then became more powerful. What parts of the Theseus myth seem to agree with history?

Building a Labyrinth

The Minoans were the first people to build mazes (or labyrinths), complicated structures in which it is easy to get lost. There are many different ways to design mazes. Here are two examples:

Use the space below to design your own maze. Below the maze explain why your maze would be difficult to get out of.

A Collection of Monsters

Cut out the pictures of the monsters and the eight verses. On a separate piece of paper, glue the descriptions below the correct picture.

Three terrible sisters are we, **1** With snakes instead of hair. One look will turn you into stone, If into our eyes you stare. **(Gorgons)**	a.
I have nine heads **2** Wild and fierce If you cut off one, then two more appear. **(Hydra)**	b.
Half a man and half a bull, **3** Imprisoned in a maze; The terror of both Greece and Crete To the end of my bloody days. **(Minotaur)**	c.
Lovely maidens of the sea, **4** Our song is pure and sweet. But do not listen, sailor, Or a terrible fate you'll meet. **(Sirens)**	d.
The head of a lion, **5** The tail is a snake, The body of a goat. What does this make? **(Chimera)**	e.
A magic winged horse **6** That no one could tame, Except Bellerophon. Do you know my name? **(Pegasus)**	f.
A woman's head, **7** A lion's middle. Only Oedipus could answer my riddle. **(Sphinx)**	g.

The Climate of Greece and the Aegean Sea

The mainland of Greece and the Greek islands have what is called a Mediterranean climate, from the name of the sea. Most of the rain falls in the winter, so the summers are very hot and dry. Westerly winds bring much rain to the western coast of Greece. However, the systems lose much of their rain in rising above the interior mountains, so the eastern regions of Greece are drier.

Here are two maps of Greece showing the average temperatures in January (winter) and July (summer). Use the maps to answer the questions below.

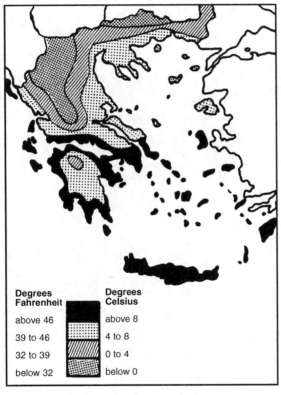

Degrees Fahrenheit		**Degrees Celsius**
above 46		above 8
39 to 46		4 to 8
32 to 39		0 to 4
below 32		below 0

January

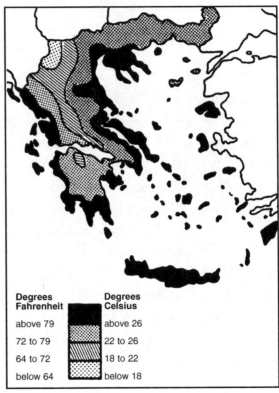

Degrees Fahrenheit		**Degrees Celsius**
above 79		above 26
72 to 79		22 to 26
64 to 72		18 to 22
below 64		below 18

July

1. What is the average difference in temperature in Athens between January and July? _____

2. Where are the warmest places in Greece in July? _____

3. Where are the warmest places in January? _____

    What pattern do you see? _____

4. What portion of Greece seems to be the coldest in both months? _____

    What pattern do you see? _____

Myth and the Emotions

We are used to thinking of gods and goddesses as beings who are very kind and good. Is the same true of the Greek gods and goddesses? Answer these questions to make your own answer to that question.

1. In this myth, which characters act in a way that you think is unfair? Name the characters and tell why.

   _____

   _____

   _____

   _____

   _____

2. Are there any characters that you feel act in a fair way? Explain.

   _____

   _____

3. Including the humans, who suffers the most in this myth? Is there any character who does not suffer?

   _____

   _____

   _____

4. From what you know about Greek myth so far, how are the gods and goddesses different from men and women?

   _____

   _____

Looking For the Hero

What is a hero? (Or a heroine?) What qualities do you think a heroic person should have? Think about these questions and list at least ten qualities.

_____   _____

_____   _____

_____   _____

_____   _____

_____   _____

Now you have had a chance to hear the stories of either Jason or Hercules, or both of them. Look at the list of characteristics you wrote. Do either, or both, of these figures possess those characteristics? Explain.

_____

_____

_____

_____

_____

_____

_____

_____

_____

_____

_____

Greek Writing

When the Greek language was first written, the lines were written from right to left. By 600 B.C. the writing was from left to write, as in English. But in between, the Greeks used an interesting technique called *boustrophedon*. Read the story below and decide what writing technique is used.

Once there was a King whose name was
yrev a saw eH .algyrhP dellac modgnik a delur eH .sadiM
greedy man. Once he did a favor for the God of Wine,
dluoc eh mih dlot dog ehT .suisynoiD saw eman esohw
have any favor that he asked for. King Midas asked that
,hguone erus dnA .dlog otni denrut eb dehcuot eh gnihtyna
thats what happened. Midas was very happy until he tried
.dlog otni denrut tI .dearb fo eceip a pu dekcip eh .tae ot
He tried to eat some grapes. They turned into gold.
slh taht ksa dna dog eht ot kcab og ot dah sadiM ,yllaniF
magic power be taken away. He had found out that his
.gniht elgnis a mih deniag ton dah deerg

Describe how this story was written.

_____

_____

_____

_____

Can you think of another way to write a story down. Try it and write it below. Show it to your classmates. Can they tell what the story is about?

_____

_____

_____

_____

_____

A Series of Duels

The Iliad is a story about war and conflict. The champions of each side challenge and duel each other as part of the battle. How many of these one-on-one duels can you list? Who were the two warriors in each duel?

Duel	Warrior 1	Warrior 2
_____	_____	_____
_____	_____	_____
_____	_____	_____
_____	_____	_____

Choose one of these duels and tell what happened. Give a few details of the struggle. Was there a clear winner?

_____

_____

_____

_____

_____

_____

Extension: Before you hear the rest of the story of *The Iliad*, make a prediction about which of the warriors will fight each other. Write it here.

_____

_____

Fact and Fiction in *The Iliad*

At one point, historians believed that nothing in *The Iliad* was true, that there was never a city named Troy, or an invasion by Greek-speaking peoples. Today, we know that certain aspects of the story really did happen. However, they did not happen in quite the way portrayed in the story. For example, in the story, the invasion lasted ten years, during which time the Greeks laid constant siege to the city. Today, historians believe that the Greeks conquest was not one invasion but several raiding parties strung out over a number of years, the last raid resulting in the sack of Troy.

Here are three more parts of the story. Use your imagination to see if you can guess what the history is behind the story.

1. HELEN

In the story, the whole war was fought because of one woman.

Your Idea

_____

_____

_____

_____

2. ACHILLES

In the story, Achilles was a half-god, who was invincible except for being vulnerable at the heel. His mother had dipped him in a sacred river that made him invulnerable, but she held him by the heel, leaving that part of his body unprotected.

Your Idea

_____

_____

_____

_____

3. THE HORSE

In the story, the Greeks trick the Trojans by building a horse and putting soldiers inside it. After the Trojans pulled the horse into the city, the soldiers came out and opened the gates.

Your Idea

_____

_____

_____

_____

Illustrating a Passage

This activity will combine a close reading of a text with artistic ability to show its meaning.

Directions:

1. As you read some portion of the story, pause and ask students if they are getting pictures in their minds as you read. Discuss how or why that happens. Have them share their mental pictures and how they help them understand the story.

2. When you have them sensitized to how they create mental pictures as they listen/read, tell them they are going to have a chance to put those pictures on paper. Explain that you will read a short passage from the text and they will listen carefully. As an example read the passage below.

   King Priam was loathe to desecrate the statue risking the wrath of the goddess. He ordered it to be hauled across the plain on rollers. When they reached the town they found that the statue was far too large to get through the gates and part of the walls had to be dismantled. The statue stuck four times but finally they got it through and rebuilt the wall behind them. Sweating in the heat of the day they laboriously began to haul the great statue up the steep street but they found the route blocked by Priam's strange but beautiful daughter Cassandra and the prophet Laocoon.

   The Legend of Odysseus. Connolly, Peter. (Oxford University Press, 1986)

3. Read the passage at least twice. If students work in teams, give them time to discuss how to lay out the picture and what elements should be in it. If you wish, have the class discuss those issues before they draw.

4. When the illustrations are done, have students write a caption for them. Compare the illustrations and find a place to post them.

5. Choose any strongly pictorial passage you feel is appropriate for your class.

The Wily Odysseus

In *The Iliad*, Achilles is the strongest and best fighter while Odysseus is considered the smartest of the Greeks. He is called "the shrewd captain," "patient man," and "great tactician," all titles which emphasize his intelligence, not his strength.

1. Look up the word "smart" in a thesaurus. Write down 10 synonyms for the word.

   _____   _____

   _____   _____

   _____   _____

   _____   _____

   _____   _____

2. There are numerous times in both *The Iliad* and *The Odyssey* that Odysseus gives evidence of his intelligence. Describe three of those times.

   a. _____

      _____

   b. _____

      _____

   c. _____

      _____

3. Are there any ways that Penelope also shows the same characteristic? Describe how she does.

   _____

   _____

   _____

Using Tableaux as a Device to Explore Meaning

This exercise will help students understand the story by making them responsible for creating a still-life of certain moments in the story.

Materials: page 25 reproduced and cut apart

Directions:

1. Show the students illustrations from one of the books you have read so far. Discuss how the illustrations help to show the incidents of the story. Discuss posture, facial expressions, the position of the hands and arms and how they all show the emotions of the different characters in the pictures.

2. Explain that each group of students will have a chance to illustrate a small part of the end of *The Odyssey* in a unique way. Each group will create a tableau for *The Odyssey*.

3. Distribute the tableau cards, one to each group. Give the groups 5-10 minutes to decide how to arrange themselves to illustrate the passage you give them.

4. Ask the other students to close their eyes while one group arranges themselves in the front of the room. Then have the students open their eyes. After the class has had a chance to look at the tableau, ask one student to read the passage.

5. Discuss the decisions the students made. What about their posture, etc., helped to express the meaning of the passage? If more than one group does a passage, discuss the differences between the presentations.

Extension: The idea of tableau can be applied to *The Iliad* if student interest merits continuing the exercise. Give students a chance to find passages themselves to present. You can also have students use tableaux as a way to explore the myths they retell as part of the Big Books exercise.

Tableaux For The Odyssey

Passage #1: *"The prince [Telemachus] climbed up to Eumaeus' cottage and found the swineherd breakfasting with an old beggar."*

Passage #2: *"All the suitors gave him [the old beggar] some food but when he reached their leader, Antoninus, he was met with a hail of abuse."*

Passage #3: *"Eurycleia knelt at his [the beggar's] feet and began to wash his legs. Suddenly her body stiffened and she let out a gasp as she felt a jagged scar above his knees. "*

Passage #4: *"The old man [the beggar] began by telling her [Penelope] that he came from Crete where he had met Odysseus at the beginning of the war. Penelope interrupted him before he went any further."*

Passage #5: *"One by one the suitors tried their skill [at bending the bow] but they all failed."*

Passage #6: *"Meanwhile the old tramp was twisting the bow lovingly between his fingers. The suitors' anger turned to laughter as they watched him."*

Passage #7: *"The king threw off his filthy cloak and seized the quiver full of arrows. . . . The first arrow struck Antoninus in the throat and his wine cup clattered to the floor."*

Passage #8: *"The suitors were trapped in the palace. . . . There could be no escape until he [Odysseus] was removed. Six of them dashed forward and hurled their spears at him."*

Passage #9: *"Urged on by Athena, Odysseus plunged into the crowd. The suitors scattered before him and he struck them down as they ran."*

Passage #10: *[Odysseus speaking:]* *" 'What other wife would refuse to embrace her husband after an absence of nineteen years,' he asked her. He then turned to the old nurse and told her to make up a separate bed for him."*

Big Book of the Gods

Making a big book will give the students an opportunity to research many of the mythological stories not covered directly in this unit.

Materials: books of Greek myths (see ideas on page 6), large lined paper, construction paper, copies of page 27

Directions:

1. Briefly explain that Greek mythology is comprised of hundreds of stories that were told and retold over centuries. What most of them have in common is that they are distinguished from other stories by how the gods and the goddesses were involved with, and interfered in, human life. Each of the Olympian deities had numerous stories told about them.

2. Form groups of three or four students to research each of the Olympians. You might also include other figures, such as Hercules, Hestia, Prometheus, the Furies, or other divine or semi-divine figures from Greek myth.

3. Have students use page 27 to help them guide their research. Aim toward each group producing two pages for the book, one page that introduces the deity and outlines his/her main characteristics, and a second page that is a retelling of a major myth in which this diety plays a major part.

Extensions:

- Challenge students to make a puppet show or readers' theater out of the myth or myths they retold.

- Many Greek deities are associated with a planet or moon in the solar system, or with a hero represented in the constellations of the night sky. Have the students research the connections between myth and science.

Research Sheet

Use this information to write your pages in the class Big Book.

Name of deity: _____

How this deity was born/was created: _____

_____

_____

What are the powers of this deity?_____

_____

_____

What are the weaknesses of this deity? _____

_____

If this deity had been a person, how would you describe him/her?

_____

_____

_____

Find a story about this deity. What is the main human character in the story? _____

_____

Does the deity bring good or evil to the human? _____

What is the main point of the story? _____

_____

Ancient Greece

by Anne Pearson

Summary

Greek civilization spanned over 1500 years and was spread throughout much of the Mediterranean region. It was a complex, diverse, and contradictory culture. Traditional histories often concentrate on dates and the lives of famous men. While this unit includes those elements, it will also include activities that will give students an understanding of the lives of ordinary people—their education, amusements, clothing, and diet.

Sample Plan

Day 1

- Daily Writing Activities
- Read pages 6-18. Emphasis: History
- The Greek World (page 61)
- Fact from Fiction (page 30)
- Begin Time Line of Greece (page 31)
- The Greek Alphabet (page 43)
- Continue Making a Greek Town
- Archaeological Simulation (page 57)

Day 2

- Daily Writing Activities
- Read pages 16-20, 54-58. Emphasis: Athens and Sparta
- Peloponnesian War Game (page 36)
- Word Webs and the Greeks (page 44)
- Finish Making a Greek Town
- Begin Portrait of a City State (page 63)

Day 3

- Daily Writing Activities
- Read pages 24-30, 60-62. Emphasis: Religion and Sports
- Begin Culminating Activity
- Continue Peloponnesian War Game
- Greek Columns (page 51)
- Continue Portrait of a City State
- Poems for Athletes (page 42)

Day 4

- Daily Writing Activities
- Pages 46-48, 58-60. Emphasis: Philosophy and Science

- Begin Pythagoras Math Centers (page 52)
- Begin presenting City State research projects
- Begin A Speech of Praise (page 45)

Day 5

- Daily Writing Activities
- Pages 30-34, 44-46. Emphasis: Daily Life
- Continue math centers (page 52)
- Finish presenting Portrait of a City State
- Continue A Speech of Praise
- Who's Got the Vote (page 34)
- Breakfast in Athens (page 67)

Day 6

- Daily Writing Activities
- Pages 50-56. Emphasis: Economic Life
- Continue math centers (page 52)
- Begin Culminating Activity
- Shapes of a Pot (page 65)
- Basic Bread (page 67)
- Closing Discussion for Time Line of Greece
- Name poem (page 42)

Day 7

- Daily Writing Activities
- Read pages 34-38. Emphasis: Children's Lives
- Finish math centers (page 52)
- A Fragment of a Pot (page 65)
- Schooling: The Art of Memory (page 68)
- Complete Culminating Activity

Overview of Activities

Setting the Stage

1. A **Time Line of Greece** will help students order the most important dates and events of Greek history. Greek history is usually divided in various ways. Here is one example: The Bronze or Heroic Age (1700-1100 B.C., from the rise of the Minoans through the Mycenaeans), The Age of Expansion (1100-500 B.C., from the Dorian Invasion to Periclean Athens), the Classical Age (500-336 B.C.E., from the Golden Age of Athens to Philip of Macedonia's victory at Chaeronea), and the Hellenistic Age (338 B.C. to 39 B.C., through Alexander's conquests until the last Greek kingdom was overthrown by Rome).
2. The **Greek Alphabet** will introduce students to the form of Greek writing. The Greek language has made a rich contribution to English. Be aware of terms borrowed from the Greek.
3. **Fact from Fiction** will introduce some facts about the Greeks that will help the students see them as the complex society that they were.

Enjoying the Book

1. The **book is divided into sections,** each dealing with aspects of Greek life. The activities designed around the sections will begin by amplifying the material in that section and then connecting it to other sections.
2. **Pictures and Words** will help students understand how books of this nature are constructed. They become aware of information in the text and information in the pictures and captions.
3. **The Greek World** will help give students a sense of the geography of the unit.
4. The Greeks of the Classical Age valued skill at public speaking. **A Speech of Praise** will give students a chance to develop their own sense of judgment about what makes a persuasive speech.

Extending the Book

1. The **Archaeology Simulation** will give students an idea of how modern scholars learn about ancient civilizations. Find out if there are any archaeological sites in your community?
2. Athens and Sparta are major players in any history of Greece. In **A Peloponnesian War Game** (page 36-40) students will exercise their skills at strategy as they learn about the major internal war of Greek history.
3. Most history of the Greeks is written from the point of view of the citizen of the city states, a small percentage of the population. **Who Has the Vote** (pages 34 and 35) will make the limitations of Greek democracy clearer.
4. **Portrait of a City State** (pages 63 and 64) will give students the opportunity to extend their knowledge of the basic political unit of Greek history.
5. Greek architecture was founded on the idea of the column. **"Greek Columns"** (page 51) will give students knowledge of the mathematical proportion of the columns.
6. **Math Centers on Pythagoras** (page 52) will help students understand the large contributions of the Greeks to the science of mathematics.
7. **The Art of Memory** will give students a taste of what school was like for the lucky few who attended in classical Greece.
8. **Food of Greece** (page 67) focuses on bread and its importance in early civilizations.
9. **Shapes of a Pot** will serve as a reminder that much of what we know about the past has been inferred from a small body of evidence.
10. **Writing Ideas** will give students a chance to express their growing knowledge of ancient Greece, its history, and culture.

Fact From Fiction: The Truth About Greece

Here are ten "statements" about Greece. Eight of them are facts and the other two are false. Read the ten and see if you can detect the impostors in the crowd. Write the word fact or fiction before the statement.

_____ 1. The most important city in ancient Greece was Athens.

_____ 2. Some of the ancient Greek civilizations became wealthy as a result of successful trade.

_____ 3. *The Iliad* and *The Odyssey* are stories about the great Mycenaean civilization of Greece.

_____ 4. The time period in which the ancient Greeks were threatened by foreign invaders, and many towns and palaces were destroyed, is known as the Bronze Age.

_____ 5. Democracy originated in the city of Athens.

_____ 6. The Greeks believed in many different gods, and would build shrines and sacrifice animals to honor them.

_____ 7. The women of ancient Greece participated freely in politics and other aspects of public life.

_____ 8. While most boys were educated in many subjects from the age of seven on, only a select few of the wealthiest young girls were taught to read and write.

_____ 9. A popular form of Greek entertainment was the many dramas performed in honor of the gods in the enormous Greek theaters.

_____ 10. The ancient sporting events were so important to the Greeks, that they would sometimes suspend wars for a brief period to allow the athletes to travel to a competition.

Introducing a Time Line of Greece

Because the book used in this section of the unit does not proceed in an overtly chronological sequence, a time line will help the students get a sense of chronological sequence in their studies.

Materials: page 32 reproduced, accountant tape or sentence strips, metersticks, markers, books on Greek history

Directions:

1. Divide the class into groups of four. Explain that they will have the opportunity to make a time line of events in the Greek world. Explain the concept of a time line if students are unfamiliar with the idea.

2. Read pages 6-7 in "The Greek World." Show the table on page 7 and explain how it divides Greek history into certain periods. Explain that the students' time lines will show the order of events in a much fuller way.

3. Ask, "How many years should each meter (100 centimeters) represent?" Point out that Greek history (if you include the Minoan) runs about 2,000 years. If each centimeter would equal 1 year, than they would need a piece of paper 20 meters long. Show the students a piece of accountant tape 20 meters long. Discuss why that is clearly too long. Help them conclude that each centimeter must equal more than one year. But how much more? Give each group time to experiment and discuss the issue.

4. Have the groups report to the class. You might wish to have the class pick the most reasonable of the ideas (e.g., 1 cm = 10 years would make a time line 2 meters long), and all follow that idea. Or let groups try different ideas.

5. Have the groups set up their time lines, marking off the centuries clearly. Post the time lines.

6. This activity will be most meaningful if you allow students to add to it daily, and if you take a few moments every day to discuss the progress.

7. Give each group a checklist (page 32) if you think that would help the class make their time lines.

Checklist for Time Line

How many of these dates can you find in your reading? When you find the date of an event, write it on the corresponding line.

_____ The Battle of Thermopylae

_____ Approximate date for the Trojan War

_____ Battle of Salamis

_____ Dorian Invasion

_____ Peloponnesian Wars

_____ Conquest of Greece by Rome

_____ The first Olympic Games

_____ The building of the Parthenon in Athens

_____ The beginning of the major Greek city states:

     _____ Athens

     _____ Sparta

     _____ Thebes

     _____ Corinth

     _____ Argos

     _____ Delos

_____ Fall of Mycenaean civilization

_____ Beginning of Delphic oracle

_____ Battle of Marathon

Birthdates and dates of death of any of the following people:

_____	Alexander the Great	_____	Solon	_____	Euripides
_____	Pythagoras	_____	Lycurgus	_____	Plato
_____	Aristarchus	_____	Pericles	_____	Pheidias
_____	Sophocles	_____	Aristotle	_____	Herodotus
_____	Sappho	_____	Themistocles	_____	Euclid
_____	Aeschylus	_____	Socrates		

These dates are just suggestions. Feel free to add any dates you find in your reading.

Information from Pictures and Text

In historical works, it is possible to get information from both the pictures and the text. In the selection that you covered today, where did the information come from?

Books read: _____   _____

Pages read: _____   _____

List three pieces of information that you learned from the text.

1. _____

    _____

2. _____

    _____

3. _____

    _____

List three pieces of information that you learned from either the pictures or the captions under the pictures.

1. _____

    _____

2. _____

    _____

3. _____

    _____

Did you see any difference in the kind of information you got through the pictures and the kind you got through the text? Explain.

_____

_____

Who Has The Vote?

Athens is known as a democracy, but the Athenian notion of democracy was quite different from ours. This exercise will give students direct knowledge of what it meant to be a citizen, or what it meant to be deprived of the rights of the citizen.

Materials: photocopies of page 35 for the class. Assuming that your class has 30 students, the following distribution would approximate the percentages of each class in Athens during the classical period:

Adult male citizens:	5 students
Adult females married to citizens:	4 students
Female children of citizens:	4 students
Male children of citizens:	5 students
Metics:	3 students
Slaves *(all ages and sexes)***:**	11 students

Directions:

1. Explain that many histories of Athens concentrate on just one section of the population, the people who were allowed to be citizens. Explain that you will show them some of the limitations of the Greek democracy.

2. Cut apart the photocopies so you have enough for the class. Randomly pass them out. Have the class read them aloud and discuss the differences in their rights. Explain that you have handed out the slips so that it will be proportionate to the numbers of each class in Athens. List the classes on the board and gather a few predictions about which one will be the most numerous.

3. Ask the students to divide so that each group stands together in a different part of the room. Discuss what the numbers mean.

Extension: Select some real-life decision that the class will be making. (You are going to give them a 20-minute free period. What do they want to do?) Allow the students who were citizens to make the decision. How do the other sections of the class feel about the process?

Who Has The Vote? *(cont.)*

Citizen

You are a male, and your father was also an Athenian citizen. (After 451 B.C. your mother's father also had to be a citizen.) At 18, you serve two years in the armed guard. After that you are always available to join the army when there is a war. You may take part and vote in the Assembly, as every citizen has the right to. You may also serve in juries. You are eligible to serve in the Council of Five Hundred, which reviews ideas before they are presented to the Assembly. You also work as a farmer, craftsman or merchant.

Citizen's Wife

You have none of the rights of your husband. Legally, you are considered his property and he may punish you as he sees fit. You spend most of your time in the house, weaving cloth and overseeing the household servants. Ordinarily, you are never seen outside the house. If your husband brings guests home, they eat in a separate room. You join your husband only for religious festivals and for plays in the city's theater.

Female Child

Some infant girls are left at the city's gates because their fathers decide they do not want to raise a girl. Other people may take these girls home, or they may starve. You do not attend school. You stay in the home and learn from your mother how to run the house and how to raise children.

Male Child

Many male children of citizens attend school for some period of time. Boys of a wealthy family may attend for many years. You receive training in athletics, reading, arithmetic and literature. You know one day you will be a citizen.

Metic

You are a person, usually a male, who was born in another city, who is allowed to live in Athens. You have no voice in the government, but you are free to run your own affairs. You may make money, and you might conceivably become quite rich. You can move back to your home city if you wish, and you can take your money along if you wish. You will never be made a citizen, no matter how successful you become.

Slave

Male or female, adult or child, you have no rights whatsoever. The kind of life you have depends solely on the kind of person who owns you. You need your master's permission to marry or have children. Your master may permit you to work for money, and (for a male) it is possible, though rare, for a slave to purchase his freedom. Other slaves are worked to death in the silver mines near Athens.

The Peloponnesian War Game

Materials: photocopies of pages 39-40 backed with tagboard to be the game board, photocopies of page 38 backed with two different colors of construction paper (laminated if possible) to be the game pieces, photocopy of page 37 (game rules), photocopy of bottom of this page to serve as recording sheets

Directions:

Make the photocopies before you introduce the game. Briefly discuss the Peloponnesian War and its main combatants. Read the rules of the game and give players a chance at the end of playing sessions to discuss their strategies.

Recording Sheets

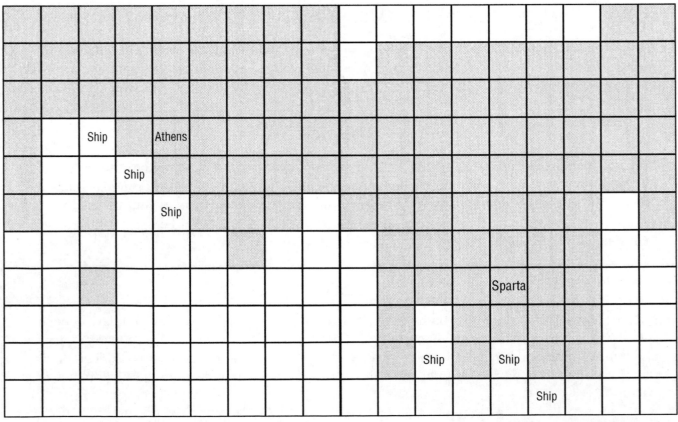

The Peloponnesian War Game *(cont.)*

Rules of the Game

1. Each side has 25 pieces to put on the game board. The pieces are distributed as follows:

- 1 Archon (King for Sparta)
- 4 Peltasts (1 pt)
- 1 Champion (5 pts)
- 1 Traitor
- 3 Knights (4 pts)
- 5 Walls
- 3 Archers (3 pts)
- 3 Triremes
- 4 Hoplites (2 pts)

1. The object of the game is to capture the other player's Archon (or King) and occupy the opposing player's city for three turns. The Archon or King has no offensive value and can be captured by any opposing piece. A champion is worth 5 points, a knight is worth 4, and so on to the peltast, who is worth one. In combat, the piece with the higher value wins. Pieces of equal value eliminate each other. The traitor has no offensive value, except when in combat with a champion or the archon which he defeats.

2. Before play begins, each player puts the pieces face down on his/her side of the board, keeping a record on the small sheet. Once play begins a player may not look at a piece to see what it is. Walls are placed in the beginning but cannot be moved. Use the recording sheet on page 36 or reproduce extra game cards for students to use.

3. Players take turns moving one piece one square in any direction. Combat is initiated by a player moving one of the pieces into the square occupied by a piece of the opposing player. At that point both pieces are turned over, and the combat is resolved as described in #1.

4. Walls can be placed anywhere within the player's own territory. Only a hoplite may breach a wall. All other pieces must go around the wall. Once a hoplite enters a square on which a wall is placed, the wall is removed.

5. Triremes may carry one piece at a time into opposing territory by sea. If a player moves a piece from a trireme into an occupied square, the combat is resolved as described in #1. Triremes may attack each other on the open sea if there is a piece with offensive value on it. Pieces on shore may not attack a piece at sea. An empty trireme is destroyed by any trireme with a piece on it. Empty triremes may not attack each other.

Game Playing Pieces

Archon

Champion
5 pts

Traitor

Knight
4 pts

Knight
4 pts

Knight
4 pts

Archer
3 pts

Archer
3 pts

Archer
3 pts

Triremes

Triremes

Triremes

Hoplite
2 pts

Hoplite
2 pts

Hoplite
2 pts

Hoplite
2 pts

Peltast
1 pt

Peltast
1 pt

Peltast
1 pt

Peltast
1 pt

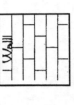
Wall

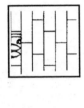
Wall

Wall

Wall

Wall

Game Board Athens

Gray = land
White = sea

	Ship		Athens				
		Ship					
			Ship				

Game Board Sparta
Gray = land
White = sea

Sparta

Ship   Ship

Ship

Daily Writing Activities

Use the activities as appropriate to your study.

Myth

1. Do you think Prometheus did the right thing? Explain your answer.

2. If you had the skill of Daedalus and could make any machine that you wished, what would you make? Tell why.

3. How does this story explain the seasons of the earth? Try to make up another story that would explain why there are different seasons on the earth.

4. Explain how magic helps tell the story of Jason and the Argonauts. If you could have a magical power, which one would you choose?

5. Do you think the Greeks were justified in attacking the Trojans for the reasons given in *The Iliad*. Why or why not?

6. Do you think this story makes war seem like a good thing to do? Why or why not? Do you know anyone who was involved in a war? What does he/she say about it?

7. Odysseus certainly has a great adventure. Imagine you went to a land where strange creatures lived and bizarre things happened. Describe your trip.

8. Both Odysseus and Penelope showed a lot of courage and determination in this story. Do you think one of them showed more or do you think they showed the same amount? Why or why not?

History

1. Imagine a whole new civilization was discovered yesterday. What would you want to know about it?

2. Would you rather live in Athens or Sparta? Justify your answer.

3. What sport do you think demands the most strength and grace? Defend your answer.

4. In Greek, the word *philosophy* means "love of wisdom." Describe a person who you think is wise. Why is that person wise?

5. What do you think of women's lives in Greece? What parts of it were unfair?

6. Before people had money with which to buy things, they used a system called barter where people traded what they grew or made for what they needed. Would such a system work today in our culture? Why or why not?

7. Do you think the life of children in ancient times was easier or harder than it is today? Defend your answer.

Poetry Ideas

Cinquains for the Gods

Cinquain is a popular five-line form of poem. Ask each student to pick one of the gods and write a simple poem according to this formula:

(one word, name of deity)	**ZEUS**
(two words, each adjectives)	Strong, wise
(three action words describing what the deity does)	Ruling, judging, creating
(Five word sentence summarizing the traits of the deity.)	He throws the bright thunderbolt.

Name Poems for Greek Figures

Choose a figure from Greek legend or history and write the name vertically down the page, one letter to a line. Use that letter to begin a sentence or phrase that describes that figure. For instance:

Sought wisdom and knowledge

Opened the minds of his students

Created the idea of a perfect society

Ranks among the world's greatest philosophers

A figure from ancient Greece

Taught his students using questions

Educator of Plato

Saw good in every person.

Poems for Athletes

Greek Olympic champions often had odes (Odes were poems that were moderate in length. They were written as poems of praise.) written about them. Ask students to pick an athlete they think is especially talented and write a poem about what they do that makes them so special.

The Greek Alphabet

The Greeks began to use an alphabet they borrowed from the Phoenicians sometime before 800 B.C. At first they wrote their letters from right to left. Later they wrote one line from right to left and then the next line was written from left to right. Eventually they settled on left to right, just as English is written.

Our modern English alphabet was modelled after the ancient Greek alphabet. Some letters still look alike, although for some the pronunciation is completely different. And the word "alphabet" itself comes from a combination of the names of the first two letters in Greek, alpha and beta.

GREEK LETTER	ENGLISH SOUND	GREEK LETTER	ENGLISH SOUND
α alpha	a as in arm	ν nu	n as in night
β beta	b as in bed	ξ xi	x as in ax
γ gamma	g as in get	ο omicron	o as in before
δ delta	d as in do	π pi	p as in pie
ε epsilon	e as in held	ρ rho	r as in ram
ζ zeta	dz as in adze	σ sigma	s as in sat
η eta	ey as in they	τ tau	t as in teach
θ theta	th as in thin	υ upsilon	u as in cube
ι iota	i as in machine	φ phi	f as in far
κ kappa	k as in kite	χ chi	lk as in elkhorn
λ lambda	l as in long	ψ psi	ps as in keeps
μ mu	m as in man	ω omega	o as in cold

Here are a few words in Greek. Try to write them into English and then see if you can tell what the word might mean. (Hint: the words will sound like an English word that might help you.)

1. λογοσ _____

2. μιχροσ _____

3. βιβλιον _____

4. κοσμοσ _____

Word Webs and the Greeks

Etymology is the study of words and their origins. Many words we know originally came from the Greek language and they were first used by the Greeks of the periods you are studying.

Psyche is one such word. It is the Greek word for "soul." It exists in many forms in our language. Look at the word wheel below:

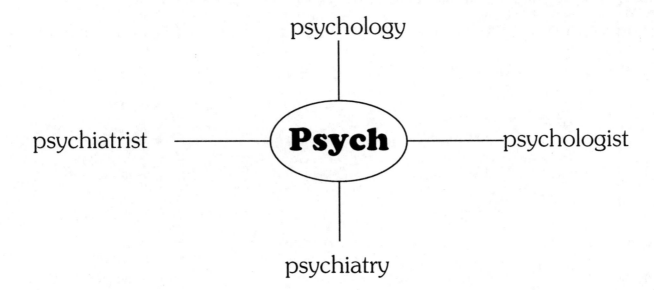

Here are three more Greek words: *ecos* meaning house, *demos* meaning people, and *polis* meaning city. Fill in the wheel for each word. Add spokes as needed.

A Speech of Praise

The Greeks valued people who were skillful at speaking. They tried to make public speaking into a science. They had names for different kinds of speeches. One was called the Encomium, meaning a speech of celebration and praise.

Write down five things or people that you think are great and deserve to be praised.

1. _____

2. _____

3. _____

4. _____

5. _____

Now pick one of those things and write down 7 reasons why what you picked is good.

1. _____

2. _____

3. _____

4. _____

5. _____

6. _____

7. _____

Using the information you wrote, practice giving a speech and then give the speech to a small group or to the whole class. What do you think makes a good speech?

Speech Evaluation

In order to judge whether someone has made a good speech, you need to know how you decide if a speech is good or not. Write down three ways that you determine if a speech is good.

1. _____

2. _____

3. _____

Share your ideas with your group. Together, choose five ways that you know if a speech is good. You will use them when you listen to the speeches of another group. After listening to the speech, you will fill out the form below to give the speaker feedback about his or her speech.

Speech Evaluation

Speaker: _____

Speech: _____

Date: _____

Here is what you did well:

_____

_____

Here is what you could improve:

_____

_____

Evaluator: _____

Persephone's Six Seeds

In the Demeter myth Persephone pays a heavy price for only eating six seeds. But these six seeds can be the basis of some math fun. All you need are six buttons, blocks, or pennies to stand for the seeds. Arrange them in a circle and number them like this:

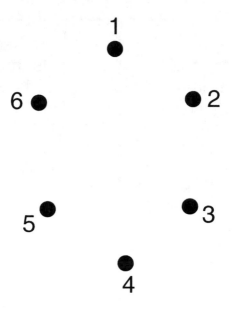

Use them to solve the following problems.

1. Imagine that Persephone is going to count out two and then eat the third seed (beginning with seed #1). She will continue this until there is only one seed left. Which seed will be left?

   _____

2. If Persephone wanted to eat seed #6 last, which seed should she start with? Make a prediction and then test the prediction.

   Prediction: _____   Test: _____

3. If Persephone had one more seed and tried the same game, what would be the order in which she ate them? Again, try predicting and then test your prediction.

   Prediction: _____

   Test: _____

Extension: Experiment with different numbers of seeds and different counting patterns. Write about what you find out.

Heracles and the Hydra

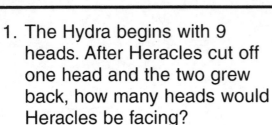

Heracles had some trouble conquering the Hydra because every time he cut off one head, two more grew in its place. So his problem got worse instead of better. You may make diagrams to solve these problems.

1. The Hydra begins with 9 heads. After Heracles cut off one head and the two grew back, how many heads would Heracles be facing?

2. Let's assume that Heracles cuts the same neck, so the two heads fall off. Four grow back. How many heads is he facing then?

3. If Heracles cuts off the same neck four times in a row, how many heads will grow from that neck alone?

4. Make a picture of Heracles facing a Hydra with 18 heads. He has made five cuts altogether. How has it happened?

Eyes of the Monster

The story of Jason contains a monster who guards a treasure by never sleeping. Another never-sleeping monster in Greek mythology was called Argus. It had 100 eyes and some of them were always open.

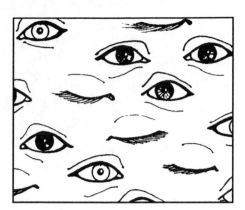

You can play a math game with Argus. You have six questions to try to find how many of Argus's eyes are open. You may ask any question that can be answered with a yes or no. Can you be sure to guess the correct number after asking six questions or fewer? Here are two games that have already been played. Read the questions and the answers and see if only one number could be the correct answer.

GAME 1

Is the number > 50?	Yes
Is the number > 90	No
Is the number < 70	Yes
Is the number > 60	No
Is the number > 55	Yes
Is the number > 58	Yes

GAME 2

Is the number in the teens?	No
Does the number have a 5 in it?	No
Is the number even?	Yes
Is the number > 50?	Yes
Is the number 88?	No
Is the number 82?	No

1. In either game did the person who was guessing eliminate every number but one number? Explain.

_____

_____

2. Which is the better list of questions? Why?

_____

_____

3. Play some games with a classmate. Did you find a strategy to always know the correct number after six questions? Explain your strategy.

_____

_____

_____

A Comb For the Cyclops

We know the Cyclops were a mythical race of giant men with only one eye. But how big is "giant"? How big was Polyphemus? Discuss this question with your group and have the recorder write your answers to these questions.

1. How big do you think Polyphemus was? _____

2. What evidence from the story do you base your estimate on?

   _____

   _____

   _____

3. If he really was as big as you say in question 1, then how big would his comb be? _____

4. Describe how you decided on your answer to question 3.

   _____

   _____

   _____

- Get a large piece of butcher paper and draw a picture of a comb that you think would be big enough for Polyphemus.

- Think of another small object that could have been in Polyphemus' cave. Make a picture of it, making it the size you think it would have been. Present your idea to the class.

Greek Columns

Most Greek buildings used one of two types of columns to support the weight of the roofs. Read the brief descriptions of each one.

THE DORIC

THE IONIC

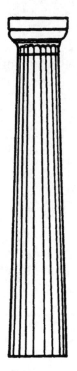

The older and simpler column is called the Doric. The shaft has no base. The height of the column is from 5 to 7 times the diameter of the base.

The Ionic is slightly thinner and more decorated than the Doric. The shaft was set on a circular or polygonal base. The height of the column is from $7\frac{1}{2}$ to $9\frac{1}{2}$ times the diameter of the base.

Get some $8\frac{1}{2}$ by 11 inch (22 cm x 28 cm) paper. Draw an example of each type of column. How will you measure them to make sure the proportions are within the ranges described above?

_____

_____

_____

Take the two columns and set them across the room. Can you tell the difference when the columns are across the room? Describe what you see.

_____

_____

Using Math Centers on Pythagoras

Pythagoras was born on the island of Samos in the Aegean Sea near the coast of what is now Turkey. He was born circa 580 B.C. He believed that one could understand the secrets of the universe by finding patterns in numbers, especially whole numbers. He was one of the first to give shape to what is now the science of mathematics. He discovered many fundamental patterns in our number system. These four centers will give students an idea about how he and his followers discovered patterns in both numbers and shapes.

Materials: An ample supply of any small manipulatives, such as pebbles, buttons, chips

Directions:

1. Set up the four centers, putting out the materials, one center for every 4-5 students.

2. Describe the history of Pythagoras as above. If the students have had experience with the Pythagorean theorem, point it out as one of his accomplishments.

3. Explain that students will have the opportunity to discover some simple patterns in numbers as Pythagoras did, using only simple materials.

4. Allow 40 minutes for the students to go through each center and make a short entry in the math log. (Reproduce as many as needed below.) The centers should be scheduled so that the students do one center on each of four days.

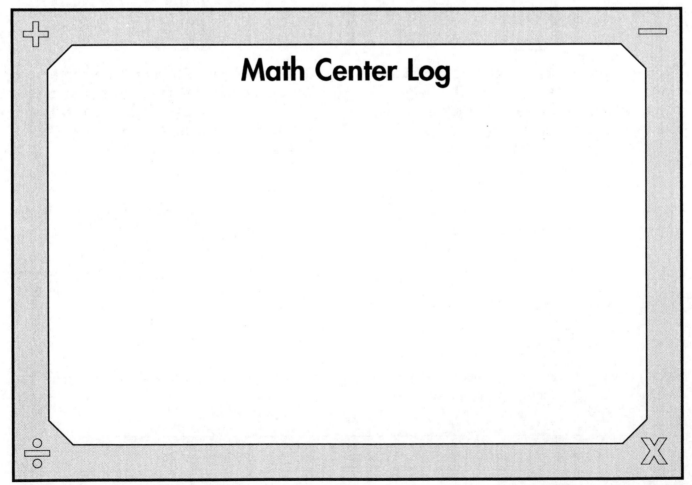

Math Center Log

Discovering Triangular Numbers

Materials: pencil, pebbles (or other small objects)

Directions:

Make the three shapes as shown below. Then continue building larger numbers until you reach a triangular number with 10 rows. Show your work by completing the table. Respond to the question and make an entry in your math log.

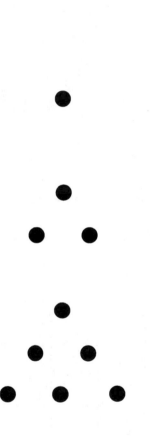

Table

Number of Rows	Number of pebbles
1	1
2	3
3	
4	
5	
6	
7	
8	
9	
10	

What pattern do you see? _____

_____

_____

Challenge: Could you find how many pebbles you need to build a triangular number with 100 rows without having to actually build one that large?

Discovering Square Numbers

Materials: pencil, pebbles (or other small objects)

Directions:

Here is the first square number: ●

Here is the next square number: ● ●
                                   ● ●

You can probably begin to see the pattern. Continue building the square numbers and complete the table.

Number of pebbles on each side	1	2	3	4	5	6	7	8	9	10
Total number of pebbles	1	4								

Look at the number of total pebbles on your table. Find how the total number of pebbles grow as the square grows. What pattern do you see?

_____

_____

_____

Discovering Oblong Numbers

Materials: pencil, pebbles (or other small objects)

Directions:

1. An oblong number is one shaped like a rectangle, whose one side is one longer than the other. Here is the first oblong number:

   Here are the second and third: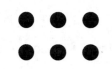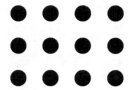

Continue with the pattern until you get one that is 9 rows tall.

Number of rows	1	2	3	4	5	6	7	8	9
Total number of pebbles	2	6	12						

Describe the pattern you see. _____

_____

_____

_____

2. Look at this pattern:

$$0 + 2, \qquad 2 + 4, \qquad 2 + 4 + 6, \qquad 2 + 4 + 6 + 8.$$

What is the pattern? _____

_____

How does it describe how to make oblong numbers? _____

_____

Discovering the Gnomon

Materials: pencil, pebbles (or other small objects)

Directions:

Here is the first gnomon:

Here are the second and third gnomons:

Use the pebbles and continue the pattern until you get a gnomon that has ten pebbles along the bottom.

Number of pebbles along the bottom	1	2	3	4	5	6	7	8	9	10
Total number of pebbles	3	5	9							

What pattern do you see? _____

_____

_____

Why must every gnomon have an odd total number of pebbles? _____

_____

_____

Can you see anything in the room that looks like a gnomon? What?

Using the Archaeology Simulation

Students will understand the process that archaeologists use to find out about the civilizations of the past as they complete this simulation.

Materials: For each group of five: ruler, tape, marker, one 9" x 13" (23 cm x 33 cm) pan, enough sand/soil to fill the pan, a small strainer, and materials to plant in the soil. The materials should be of three varieties—simple wood and ceramic pieces (such as toothpicks, bits of wooden implements and pots), simple metal objects (nails, keys, paper clips), and objects showing advanced technology (capacitors, plastic, printing), small spoons and toothpicks.

Directions:

1. Briefly discuss how we have found out about the Greeks and other early civilizations. Introduce the idea of digging in the earth and making conclusions based on what you find there.

2. Before the class, prepare the pans. You might make two or three samples of each mix: 1) one mix being only wood and ceramic objects, 2) one a mixture of wood/ceramic and metal objects, and 3) one a mixture of metal/high tech items. You might include some very small items to see if the students are thorough enough to find them. Divide the class into groups of five and introduce the pans. Include seven to ten objects for each pan.

3. Challenge the students to find out what kind of civilization left the remains in these pans. Go over the directions on page 58 and model how to map the objects that they find. The mapping should be recorded so that the students can tell where and how deeply in the soil each artifact was found.

4. Divide the responsibilities as follows: one recorder, one reporter, and three diggers. Have the diggers use small spoons and toothpicks. Give the students 30-40 minutes to explore the pan. Encourage the groups not to hurry. Have the groups report to the class and discuss their conclusions.

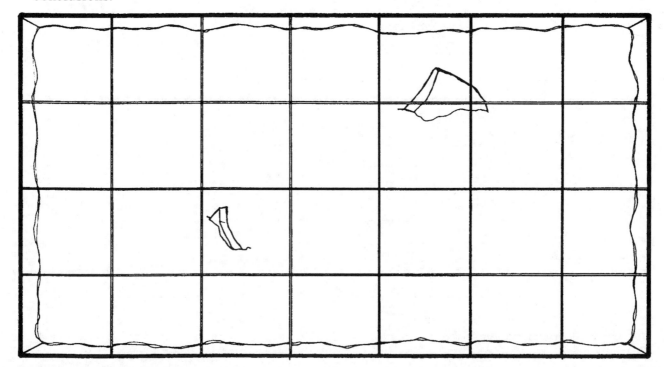

Archaeology Recording Sheet

Materials: ruler, tape, marker, pan, pens of two colors

Directions:

1. Measure and mark off the pan in inches. Draw a top view of the pan in the outline below. Take out the sand a little at a time and record on your drawing paper where you found each object. Use one color pen for objects you found near the top. Use another color for those you found near the bottom.

2. Identify each object:

a. _____   f. _____

b. _____   g. _____

c. _____   h. _____

d. _____   i. _____

e. _____   j. _____

Archaeological Conclusions

After you have completed recording your findings answer these questions.

1. What patterns do you see in the objects you found?

_____

_____

_____

_____

2. Do you see changes in the objects that you found near the bottom and those you found near the top? Explain.

_____

_____

_____

_____

3. What type of society left the objects you found? Describe that society.

_____

_____

_____

_____

Investigating Three Grains

Demeter is the goddess of the harvest, and all grains were holy to her. Sacrifices were made to her when the grain was planted and when it was harvested. Your teacher will have samples of three grains for you to investigate. Find the following information for each.

Grain #1   Name: _____

Make a picture here: Write a brief description:

_____

_____

_____

Measure three grains. How many millimeters long are they?

_____   _____   _____

Grain #2   Name: _____

Make a picture here: Write a brief description:

_____

_____

_____

Measure three grains. How many millimeters long are they?

_____   _____   _____

Grain #3   Name: _____

Make a picture here: Write a brief description:

_____

_____

_____

Measure three grains. How many millimeters long are they?

_____   _____   _____

The Greek World

Greek city states were scattered across the eastern Mediterranean. Use the map on page 62 and the clues below to locate the major cities in Greece and in the eastern Mediterranean.

NAME OF CITY	CLUE
Thebes	Northwest of Athens.
Samos	Just off coast of Asia Minor on one of the larger islands.
Athens	East of Corinth, on a peninsula.
Syracuse	On the island of Sicily.
Pylos	In the southwestern corner of the Peloponnesus.
Sparta	East of Pylos.
Argos	In the Peloponnesus, between Sparta and Corinth.
Mytilene	On the island of Lesbos, west of Pergamum.
Corinth	Located on an isthmus north of Sparta.
Rhodes	Island south of Asia Minor.
Miletus	In Asia Minor, southeast of Samos.
Alexandria	In Africa, at the mouth of the Nile.
Delphi	North of the Gulf of Corinth, west of Thebes.
Pergamum	The northernmost city in Asia Minor.
Cyrene	In Africa, west of Alexandria.
Delos	Small island in the Aegean.

Map of Greece

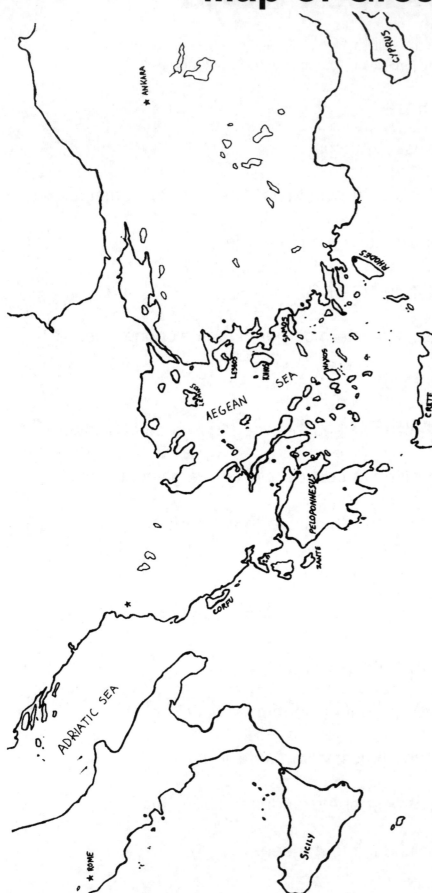

Portrait of a City State

The fundamental political unit in ancient Greece was not the nation, as it is in the 20th century, it was the city state. Greek history is normally told from an Athenian point-of-view, and this exercise can help balance that view.

Materials: Large poster board, construction paper, or any other material that groups need to present the information that they find. It is very important to have a number of books about ancient Greece for this activity.

Directions:

1. Ask the students if they think there was a nation called Greece in ancient times. Discuss the fact that there wasn't. The Greeks did not think of themselves as a nation. They gave their allegiance to the city where they lived. The country we now call Greece is a collection of city states.

2. Explain that Athens is the most famous of the city states for a variety of reasons. It was often politically and economically the most powerful. A large proportion of artists and writers of the era were born there. But it was certainly not the only city state to make contributions. Tell the students they will have the chance to find out about the other city states and what happened there.

3. See how many city states the students can name. Make a list on the board. Pass out page 61 and complete the list. Divide the students into groups of four and let them discuss which city state they want to study. Ask for second and third choices. See the map on page 62 for the location of the city states. Try to get all the city states represented. You might give two groups each to Athens and Sparta.

4. Allow three or four 45-minute sessions for students to gather and organize what they find. Give each group 4-8 minutes to present their information to the class.

5. There will be some overlap in information between this presentation and the time lines that the students are doing. Encourage students to use the time lines as one way to get information.

Research Sheets for City States

Name of city state: _____

Location: _____

Population: _____

Tell about the beginning of this city state. _____

_____

_____

_____

Tell about the famous people who came from this city state. _____

_____

_____

_____

Tell about the events that happened in this city state. _____

_____

_____

_____

_____

Are there ruins of this city state that have been explored? Tell about them. _____

_____

Ancient Greek Art Ideas

Try some of these art ideas to simulate some ancient Greek art experiences.

The Shields of *The Iliad*

Greek shields were sometimes decorated with intricate designs. Two are described in *The Iliad*. Get a translation of *The Iliad* and read the two passages. Agamemnon's armor is described in Book 11, lines 15-48, and Achilles' shield is described in Book 18, lines 483-619. As an extension, you might give an artistic student the description of Agamemnon and ask him/her to make a poster of what he might have looked like.

Grain Art

Get a variety of grains and beans. Students can make pictures by gluing the grains onto a sheet of paper. Encourage students to choose a scene from a Greek myth they have read.

Eyes Everywhere

The picture of the cup and the accompanying caption explains the importance of the eye as a symbol in Greek art. How many ways are there to paint/draw the eye? See how many ways students can create a design using eyes. Display them on a board.

Eyes were symbolic in ancient Greek art. They were thought to give objects life and power.

Shapes of a Pot

Show the variety of Greek pots in *Ancient Greece*, (page 49). Show the many shapes and uses of Greek pots. Give students paper and pencils and markers and see if they can create and decorate their own shapes for pots. Ask them to explain their use.

A Fragment of A Pot

Often archaeologists are able to reconstruct whole objects from just a fraction. "Shapes of a Pot" has given students an idea of the variety of Grecian pots. Reproduce the fragment to the right and challenge the students to pick a variety of pot and reconstruct the whole pot

Ancient Greek Art Ideas *(cont.)*

Red On Black

Greek pottery after the 5th century B.C. showed red painting on a black background. You can get the same effect in a painting by first copying the amphora on this page. Have the students cover the page with a rusty red layer of crayon (mix red and orange). Cut out the amphora. Then cover it with a mixture of black tempera and vegetable shortening. Allow the black layer to almost dry. Then use any sharp point (pencil, end of a paper clip) to make the drawings. The rusty red layer will show through. Encourage students to imitate the Greek style.

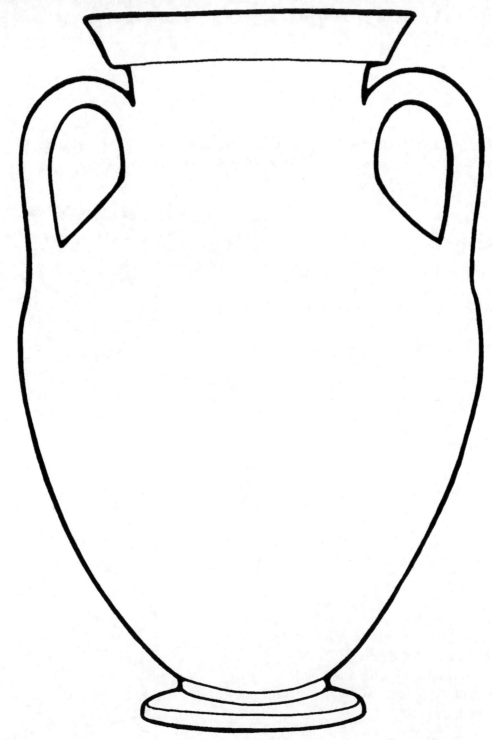

Food of Greece
Ancient Greece

Breakfast in Athens

The most common Greek breakfast consisted simply of hard bread dipped in wine. You can simulate an ancient Greek breakfast by buying some hard crusted unsliced bread and some grape juice and serving it to the class in the morning. Ask them if it seems like it would be a good, nourishing breakfast. Ask students to compare it with what they usually eat.

Modern Greece

Basic Bread

Here is a recipe for a ring-shaped bread called Koulora.

Ingredients:

- 2 cups (500 mL) scalded milk
- 2 tablespoons (30 mL) oil
- ¼ cup (60 mL) lukewarm water
- 4 cups (1 L) flour
- 3 tablespoons (45 mL) sesame seeds
- 2 tablespoons (30 mL) honey
- 1 package dry yeast
- 1 teaspoon (5 mL) salt
- 1 egg white, slightly beaten

Put the milk, 1 tablespoon (15 mL) oil, and the salt into a bowl. Dissolve the yeast into the water while milk cools. When the milk is warm pour the yeast into the milk. Then gradually beat in the flour. Turn the mixture onto a lightly floured board. Knead until smooth. Shape it into a ball and cover with the rest of the oil. Cover and let it rise in a warm place until it has doubled (1-2 hours). Punch it down and knead it for another ten minutes. Roll it into a cylinder about 2 feet (60 cm) long. Brush the egg white onto the top and sprinkle with sesame seeds and a dash of salt. Use a tube pan to bake the bread if you have one. If not, form the dough into a ring and allow the dough to rise a second time (about ½ an hour). Bake at 375°F (190°C) for 60-80 minutes, or until the top is golden.

The Art of Memory

You have heard in today's reading that boys in Greek schools were expected to memorize long sections of poetry, many times from *The Iliad* or *The Odyssey*. In fact, for many centuries these poems were never written down. They were memorized, and repeated by many storytellers.

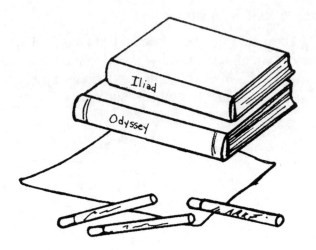

Your teacher will supply you with translations of *The Iliad* and/or *The Odyssey*. Your assignment is to choose 10-20 lines of one of the poems and memorize them. How will you go about this? You will need to practice! Recite the lines over and over again. When you think you know them say them out loud. You may need to have someone help you. When you are finished, answer these questions about your section.

What happens in the section that you decided to memorize?

_____

_____

Describe what you did to memorize the section.

_____

_____

_____

_____

What happened when you tried to recite your lines to the class? How did you do?

_____

_____

_____

_____

Putting On The Olympics

A Very Practical Project

Athletics were a very important aspect of Greek life. To them a sound philosophy was incomplete without a due regard for a healthy body, and physical beauty for them was neither shallow nor superficial. In this activity students will learn about the Olympics by running a small version of their own.

Directions:

1. Begin a discussion about the Olympics and what they mean to the students. If you have any local angle to the modern Olympics, use it to begin the discussion.

2. Turn the discussion to the idea of having an athletic event like the Olympics at your school. What would be the difficulties? Who would take part in it?

3. Explain that if the students are going to set up their event, they should know something about the original Olympics. Use "Fact Sheet on the Olympics" (page 70) to help students provide a background for themselves.

4. In a whole class context, set up some parameters for the event. How many classes will participate? If you decide to keep it small, then students may choose to compete in any event they are not themselves administering. The class might also decide to open the events to all the classes of your grade or to multiple grades.

5. Divide the students into five groups, one to be in charge of each event. Use "Event Information" (page 75) and the "Events Ladder" (page 76) to keep track of how the groups are proceeding.

6. If other classes are to be involved, arrange time for students to introduce their event, the technique involved, and how to sign up to the other classes. Make posters and publicize the event. You might decide to hold the event all on one day, or on five separate days, like the original games.

Fact Sheet on The Olympics

Use the encyclopedia and other books to answer these questions about the ancient Greek Olympics.

1. What was the date of the first Olympics? _____

2. The Olympics were dedicated to one of the gods or goddesses. Which one? _____

3. There were five parts in the event known as the pentathlon. Name them.

   _____

   _____

   _____

   _____

   _____

4. There were footraces in every Olympics. Did some Olympics feature other kinds of races? Name them.

   _____

   _____

5. How often were the ancient Olympics held?_____

6. When was the last ancient Olympics held?_____

7. The Olympics were not the only famous ancient athletic games held in Greece. There were three other major competitions. Name them.

   _____

   _____

   _____

8. Given your answers to #1 and #6, how long were the Greek games held? _____

9. If the Olympics were never cancelled, how many ancient Olympic games would have been held? How does that compare with the modern Olympics?

   _____

   _____

Event #1—50 Yard or 50 M Dash

History

The shortest race in the ancient Olympic games was actually about 200 yards (180 m) long. The Greeks called that distance a "stade," and our word for stadium comes from that word. The runners began in a standing position, with one foot slightly ahead of the other. They raced in straight lines from one end of the stadium to another. To mark the finish line, the Greeks set posts upright in the ground.

Setting Up Your Events

Your group will need to find a place on the playground where 4-6 people can run 50 yards or 50 meters. You might use chalk or tape to show the lanes. To make the starting place, which the Greeks called a "balbis," use tape or chalk to make a rectangle about 18 inches (46 cm) wide. Divide the balbis into 3 equal sections. See diagram at right.

The runners should have one foot on each of the two lines so one foot will be slightly ahead of the other.

Talk to a physical education teacher or do some research about how a runner should warm up before running a race. If you make presentations to other classes about this event, make sure you include the proper way to warm up as part of your presentation.

Rules of the Events

1. Divide the racers into heats, up to six in each heat. Tell the runners that they must not start until the signal is given. (The signal may be anything you want.) The runners must stay in their lanes, or be disqualified.

2. As in all Greek Olympic events, the fastest runner was not always the winner. The judges could give the prize to a slower runner if that runner ran with more grace and beauty. Speed was not everything to them. Whatever you decide, make sure that the contestants know how you will decide before they begin the event.

Event #2—100 Yard or 100 M Dash

The ancient Greeks did not run the 100 yard (100 m) dash. Their shortest race, called a "stade," was 200 (180 m) yards. Follow the rules as for the 50 yard (50 m) dash.

Event #3—Wrestling

History

Wrestling was one of the original Olympic events. The two contestants began in a standing position and wrestled until one gave up or was unable to go on. Later, a brutal sport called "pankration," a combination of boxing and wrestling, was introduced. Throwing an opponent to the ground gave a wrestler one point. The match was over when three points were scored by one wrestler. There were no weight classes in Greek wrestling.

Setting Up Your Event

Wrestling is a dangerous sport requiring great skill from the participants. The students in your class or school will not have the time to become expert enough to compete without danger, so here is a simpler form of wrestling.

You do not need any special ring or square for your event, although you may wish to trace two feet right next to each other (one's toes next to the other's heel) as a mark for the wrestlers. Use form #1 on the Events Ladder (page 76) to record the results of the matches. Group the wrestlers into pairs. Have the winners of each group then compete against each other.

Rules of the Game

1. Ask the participants to stand with the outside of their right feet touching. They should also be shaking hands with their right hands.

2. At your signal they begin pulling and pushing. They may move their left foot in either direction. They may push and pull with their right hands, but they must continue to clasp hands. They may not touch each other with their left hands. The winner is the one who makes the other move his/her right foot first.

3. As in all Greek Olympic events, the wrestler who won the three matches was not always the winner. The judges could give the prize to a another wrestler if he showed more grace and beauty. Whatever you decide, make sure that the contestants know how you will decide before they begin the event.

Event #4—The Long Jump

History

The modern long jump allows jumpers a very long runway to build up speed. Modern jumpers jump into a pit, and they are not required to land on their feet. The ancient Greek long jump was quite different.

There was only a small runway for the ancient athletes. A jump was disqualified if they did not land entirely and only on their feet. The Greeks held small weights in their hands called "halteres." As they jumped they swung their arms forward, so that the two weights helped them to jump further. One writer claimed that a jumper was able to jump over fifty feet! We don't know how far the ancient Greeks were able to jump with their method, but fifty feet (15 m) is almost surely an exaggeration.

Setting Up Your Event

1. The Greeks allowed a space of about 15 feet (4.5 m) for the jumpers to run before jumping. You might measure off that distance or have the jumpers jump from a standing start. The Greeks allowed the halteres to be any weight and shape whatsoever. If you decide to allow the jumpers to use them, get two objects that weigh between one-half pound and two pounds (225 g).

2. Use tape or string to measure a rectangle approximately 5' x 15' (1.5 m x 4.5 m). If you wish to have a runway, mark off another box approximately 5' (1.5 m) square. See drawing below:

Rules of the Game

1. If you are going to allow halteres, introduce them to the contestants a week or two before the event so they can practice with them at recesses. (Try the event yourself so you know what it is like.)

2. Give each jumper three attempts. If any part of a jumper's toes touch the fault line, then that jumper is disqualified. Be very clear about that with contestants before the event begins.

Event #5—The Discus

History

The discus of the ancient events was made usually of metal, although it was permissible to use one made of stone. It could weigh anywhere from five to eight pounds or 2.25 kg. The contestants would often engrave messages on their discus, especially if the discus had won the event for them.

We are used to seeing discus throwers spin around, using the momentum of their bodies to give the discus more force. The ancient Greeks, it is believed, faced the direction in which they would make their throw, swung the discus back and forth and then took one forward step to make their throws.

Setting Up Your Event

1. Modern discus throwers make their throws from within a circle. The ancient Greeks made throws from within a rectangular area called a "balbis." The contestant could begin and end his throw from anywhere inside the rectangle. Stepping outside the area disqualified that throw. You may choose either shape for your event.

2. Use tape on the playground to make your throwing area. You will also need something to use as a discus. A frisbee is the most similar shape, but most frisbees are too light to be thrown as a discus. You might mold some clay around the inside lip of the frisbee to make it somewhat heavier. You will also need a string with meters marked and one meterstick to measure the distance of each throw.

Rules of the Event

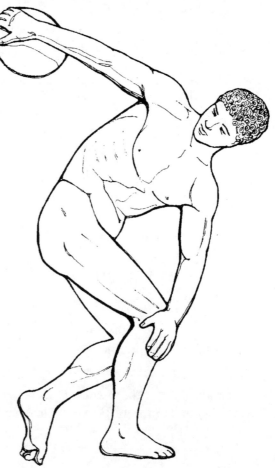

1. Allow the throwers to use any method that they wish. However, make it clear that the discus must be held with the fingers curled around the edge of the discus. (See illustration.) Do not allow the contestants to throw the discus like a frisbee. Allow three throws per contestant.

2. As in other events, the ancient Greeks also judged the contestants by the beauty of their throw. Someone who threw the discus the longest distance did not always win the event, if the judges felt that another contestant threw with more grace and beauty. You may judge as you decide, but make sure the contestants are told how you will decide before they compete.

Event Information

Name of event: _____

Names of team members:

_____ _____ _____

_____ _____ _____

_____ _____ _____

1. What materials do you need for your event?

    _____

    _____

2. Make a drawing of where in the school yard you will hold your event.

3. How will you judge the event? _____

    _____

    _____

Events Ladder

#1

#2   **Heat**   **Finals**

#3 **1st Attempt**   **2nd Attempt**   **3rd Attempt**

Making a Greek Town

Amid the swirl of mythological stories and historical events, this bulletin board will help students gain an understanding of daily life in the Greek polis. This activity will involve drawing, research, labeling and captioning.

Materials: encyclopedia and other reference books about the everyday life of the Greeks (see bibliography), sentence strips, butcher paper, pencils, scissors

Directions:

1. Cover a large bulletin board with butcher paper. Explain that although each Greek town had its own unique appearance, most Greek towns had strong similarities. Introduce the bulletin board as a way of representing what a typical Greek town might have looked like.

2. Give students time to look in their books for pictures of towns and buildings. Discuss what the buildings were called. Discuss what parts show up in more than one picture. Keep a list of the names on the board.

3. When you have pictures of houses and other buildings, have some of the students draw them on the butcher paper. You might have them practice on scratch paper first. Encourage them to use pencil so mistakes can be fixed. Encourage them to draw "cut away" views so interior parts of buildings can later be labeled and captioned.

4. As the pictures are being drawn, have other students research and write captions onto sentence strip paper.

5. This activity will be most useful if the class sees it as something to add on to as they continue to read and learn more about the life of the Greeks. One idea for closure is to invite another class learning about Greece into the room and present the bulletin board and the results of the class research.

PARTICIPANT IN THE GAMES

This certifies that

_____

competed in the

_____

event on

_____

(date)

Great!

Bibliography

Alexander, Beatrice. *Famous Myths of the Golden Age.* (California State Department of Education, 1969).

Coolidge, Olivia. *The Golden Days of Greece.* (Thomas Crowell Company, 1968).

D'aulaire, Ingri and Edgar. *D'Aulaires' Book of Greek Myths.* (Doubleday, 1962).

Durant, Will. *The Life of Greece.* (Simon and Schuster, 1966).

Espeland, Pamela. *King Midas.* (Carolrhoda Books, 1980).

Espeland, Pamela. *The Story of Cadmus.* (Carolrhoda Books, 1980).

Evslin, Bernard & Hoopes. *The Greek Gods.* (Scholastic, 1966).

Evslin, Bernard et. al. *Heroes & Monsters of Greek Myths.* (Scholastic, 1967).

Fisher, Leonard Everett. *The Olympians.* (Holiday House, 1984).

Gay, Kathlyn. *Science in Ancient Greece.* (Franklin Watts, 1988).

Homer. *The Iliad.* Translated by Robert Fitzgerald. (Anchor, 1974).

Hutton, Warwick. *Theseus and the Minotaur.* (Margaret K. McElderry Books, 1989).

Johnston, Norma. *Pride of Lions.* (Atheneum, 1979).

Naden, Corinne. *Pegasus, the Winged Horse.* (Troll Associates, 1981).

Palmer, Robin. *Centaurs, Sirens and Other Classical Creatures.* (Henry Z. Walck, Inc., 1969).

Powell, Anton. *Greece.* (Franklin Watts, 1987).

Quennell, Marjorie & C.H.B. *Everyday Things in Ancient Greece.* (G.P. Putnam's Sons, 1962).

Rutland, Jonathan. *See Inside an Ancient Greek Town.* (Warwick Press, 1986).

Untermeyer, Louis. *The Firebringer.* (M. Evans and Co., 1968).

Valens, Evans G. *The Number of Things.* (E.P. Dutton, 1964).

Answer Key

Page 13

Answers should compare the complicated places with the labyrinth, the minotaur with the bull sports of Crete, and/or the sending of Greek youths with the idea that the Mycancaens were weaker than the Cretan Empire.

Page 15
1. d
2. f
3. b
4. g
5. c
6. a
7. e

Page 16
1. 18° C. (64.4° F)
2. Along the coasts.
3. Southern coast & along Gulf of Corinth. Near the water.
4. The interiors. Places closer to water are generally warmer.

Page 20

Answers may include Paris vs. Menelaus, Diomedes vs. Pandarus, Pandarus vs. Menelaus, Aeneas vs. Diomedes, Ares vs. Diomedes, Ajax and Hector, Hector vs. Diomedes

Page 21
1. The war was probably fought over trade and Control of the Straits connecting the Aegean and the Black Sea.
2. The armor of the time covered much of the body, but the heel was unprotected.
3. Attackers used a horse-like machine to protect them as they tried to knock down the walls of a city.

Page 30

1. Fact	6. Fiction
2. Fact	7. Fact
3. Fact	8. Fact
4. Fiction	9. Fact
5. Fact	10. Fact

Page 43

1. Logos	2. milkos
3. biblio	4. kosmos

Page 47
1. 1
2. 6, of course
3. 3, 6, 2, 7, 5, 1, 4

Page 48

1. 10	2. 12	3. 16

4. He cut a neck 3 times. He cut two others once.

Page 49
1. No. In #1, it could be 59 or 60. (In #2 it could be any even number except 88 and 82 and any of the even 50's.)
2. #1. It eliminated more numbers.
3. If students begin by eliminating 50 numbers, & continue eliminating 1/20 of the remaining numbers, they will be left with 1 number.

Page 53

# of pebbles

1, 1	2, 3	3, 6	4, 10	5, 15
6, 21	7, 28	8, 3	6 9, 45	10, 55

Page 54

1, 1	2, 4	3, 9	4, 16	5, 25
6, 36	7, 49	8, 64	9, 81	10, 100

Page 55

1, 2	2, 6	3, 12	4, 20	5, 30
6, 42	7, 56	8, 72	9, 90	

Page 56

1, 3	2, 5	3, 7	4, 9	5, 11
6, 13	7, 15	8, 17	9, 19	10, 21

Page 70
1. 776 B.C.
2. Zeus
3. Javelin, Discus, Wrestling, Broad Jump, 200 yard dash
4. Horse racing, Foot races with armor
5. Every 4 years, like the modern
6. 394 B.C.
7. Isthmian, Nemean, Pythian
8. 41 to 70 years
9. 265 times. Modern Olympics have been held _____ times.